WELLSTONE
INTERNATIONAL SCHOOL
1006 W. LAKE STREET
MPLS., MN. 55408

I Like Corn

By Robin Pickering

Children's Press
A Division of Grolier Publishing
New York / London / Hong Kong / Sydney
Danbury, Connecticut

Photo Credits: Cover, pp. 7, 9, 11, 13, 15, 17, 19, 21 by Thaddeus Harden; p. 5 © Index Stock Photography, Inc.

Contributing Editor: Jennifer Ceaser
Book Design: Nelson Sa

Visit Children's Press on the Internet at:
http://publishing.grolier.com

Library of Congress Cataloging-in-Publication Data

Pickering, Robin.
　I like corn / by Robin Pickering.
　　p. cm. — (Good food)
　Includes bibliographical references and index.
　Summary: Describes corn on the cob and several other foods made from corn.
　ISBN 0-516-23084-0 (lib. bdg.) — ISBN 0-516-23009-3 (pbk.)
　1 .Cookery (Corn)—Juvenile literature. 2. Corn—Juvenile literature. [1. Corn.] I. Title.

　TX809.P53 2000
　641.6'315—dc21

00-024373

Contents

Do you know what corn is?

Corn is a **vegetable**.

Corn grows on tall plants.

5

This is an ear of corn.

An ear of corn isn't for hearing.

It's for eating!

7

When you eat corn, you are eating **kernels**.

Kernels are the soft **seeds** of the corn.

9

Kernels grow on a **cob**.

The cob is the hard center of an ear of corn.

I like to eat corn on the cob.

I eat my corn on the cob with butter.

13

Cornmeal and water can make a batter.

Cornmeal is dry, ground-up corn.

We mix beans and **peppers** into the batter.

We use the mix to make tamales (te-**mah**-leez).

I wrap the mix in **husks**.

Husks are the green leaves that cover corn.

Then my mom cooks the tamales in water.

Look at all the ways there are to eat corn!

How do you like to eat corn?

New Words

cob **(kob)** the hard center of an ear of corn

cornmeal (**korn**-meel) dry corn that has been ground up

husks **(husks)** green leaves that fold around corn

kernels (**ker**-nlz) corn seeds

peppers (**pep**-erz) red vegetables with a hot taste

seeds **(seedz)** the small parts of plants that grow into new plants

tamales (te-**mah**-leez) a food made from cornmeal, peppers, and beans

vegetable (**vej**-teh-bul) the part of a plant that you can eat

To Find Out More

Books

Corn is Maize: The Gift of the Indians
by Aliki
Harper & Row

Kids' First Cookbook
by the American Cancer Society
American Cancer Society

The Tortilla Factory
by Gary Paulsen
Harcourt and Brace

Web Sites

Kids CORNer
http://www.ohiocorn.org/kids/default.htm
This site has fun activities to help you learn about ways that corn is used.

The Maize Page
http://www.ag.iastate.edu/departments/agronomy/general.html
Learn the basic facts about corn. This site also answers questions about corn.

Index

About the Author
Robin Pickering is a writer, editor, and yoga instructor living in Brooklyn, New York.

Reading Consultants
Kris Flynn, Coordinator, Small School District Literacy, The San Diego County Office of Education

Shelly Forys, Certified Reading Recovery Specialist, W.J. Zahnow Elementary School, Waterloo, IL

Peggy McNamara, Professor, Bank Street College of Education, Reading and Literacy Program